W9-ACR-313

Young Entrepreneurs

Run Your Own
Yard Sale

Emma Carlson Berne

PowerKiDS press™

New York

Published in 2014 by The Rosen Publishing Group, Inc.
29 East 21st Street, New York, NY 10010

First Edition

Editor: Joanne Randolph
Book Design: Andrew Povolny
Photo Research: Katie Stryker

Photo Credits: Cover, pp. 24, 29 David Sacks/Lifesize/Thinkstock; p. 4 Joe McNally/Hulton Archive/Getty Images; p. 5 Kellie L. Folkerts/Shutterstock.com; p. 6 Ilike/Shutterstock.com; p. 7 Paul McKinnon/Shutterstock.com; p. 9 Fred Sweet/Shutterstock.com; p. 10 Romakoma/ Shutterstock.com; p. 11 Atlaspix/Shutterstock.com; p. 15 Michael C. Gray/Shutterstock. com; p. 16 Lilya Espinosa/Shutterstock.com; pp. 17, 20, 23 iStockphoto/Thinkstock; p. 18 Mat Hayward/Shutterstock.com; p. 19 Steve Debenport/E+/Getty Images; p. 22 PhotoObjects.net/Thinkstock; p. 24 Pressmaster/Shutterstock.com; p. 27 Real Deal Photo/ Shutterstock.com.

Library of Congress Cataloging-in-Publication Data

Berne, Emma Carlson.
  Run your own yard sale / by Emma Carlson Berne. — First edition.
     pages cm. — (Young entrepreneurs)
  Includes index.
  ISBN 978-1-4777-2919-9 (library) — ISBN 978-1-4777-3008-9 (pbk.) —
ISBN 978-1-4777-3079-9 (6-pack)
  1. Garage sales—Juvenile literature. 2. Young businesspeople—Juvenile literature.
  3. Entrepreneurship—Juvenile literature. I. Title.
  HF5482.3.B475 2014
  381'.195—dc23
                                           2013028071
Manufactured in the United States of America

CPSIA Compliance Information: Batch #W14PK2: For Further Information contact Rosen Publishing, New York, New York at 1-800-237-9932

Contents

Businesses Aren't Just for Adults!   4

How About a Yard Sale?   6

Let's Make a Plan   8

A Budget Is Key   12

Advertise! Advertise!   16

Supply Yourself   20

Power in Numbers   24

Your Very Own Yard Sale   26

Are You Ready?   30

Glossary   31

Index   32

Websites   32

Businesses Aren't Just for Adults!

Have you ever dreamed of having your own business? Maybe you thought, "Someday when I'm an adult, I can." Well, you can actually have your own business right now. You can be an **entrepreneur** at any age. An entrepreneur is a person who creates, organizes, and manages a business.

Bill Gates, shown here as a young man, is a famous entrepreneur. He started the company Microsoft with his partner Paul Allen in 1975. He is now one of the wealthiest men alive.

Not everyone will be as successful as Bill Gates, but anyone with a good business idea who is willing to work hard can be a successful entrepreneur.

To start your very own business, you will want to follow some key steps. First, you must find a need for a product or service. Then make a business plan to fulfill that need. Once you have a good plan in place, you are ready to open and run the business. If you manage your business well, you should soon start making money. For every entrepreneur, young or old, that is the best part!

How About a Yard Sale?

One of your first steps as a young entrepreneur is to look around you. Is there a need or a want in your community, at your school, or among your friends that you could fulfill? Can you think of a business that would supply your market with the need or want you identified? If there is a demand for a product or service, then that is a great start to a new business.

Have your friends help you brainstorm, or come up with some ideas for businesses. Do some research on your best ideas at the library or on the Internet.

You may see that yard sales in your neighborhood are popular. If you plan ahead, a yard sale can be a simple way to make some money.

People like to feel they are getting a good value when they buy things. For some kinds of products, buying used items can save a lot of money. In this book, you'll learn how to organize and run your own yard sale, at which you can sell used household items, clothing, and toys.

Let's Make a Plan

All good businesses have business plans. These are written documents that lay out where, when, and how you will start and run your business.

For your yard sale business plan, think about the "where" first. Will you hold your yard sale in your own yard or driveway? Perhaps you don't have a good spot on your own property. You can ask a neighbor if you can hold the sale on her lawn and then give her part of the **profits**. Maybe your church or school would let you hold the yard sale in their parking lot. Make sure that whatever spot you choose is big enough for people to move around tables of sale items easily. Think also about whether your site is a place where lots of people who might stop for your sale drive by. If your neighborhood is out of the way, you might want to think about asking to use a more public and well-traveled place for your sale.

Write your business plan down or type it on a computer. Make a list of the things you will need to get started and keep track of what you have already done.

FF 95594731 A

If you live in a home with a good-sized yard and plenty of parking on the street, this can be a simple and convenient place to hold your sale.

Next, consider the "when" of your yard sale. You want to attract the maximum number of people, so think about when most people are home from work or school. Your best bet is probably to hold your sale on a weekend.

Tip Central

Don't forget a rain plan! Will you set a rain date? Can you move into a garage or a shed if there is rain on the big day? Good business owners always plan for these kinds of possibilities.

Don't forget the "how" of your yard sale. How will you get the items you want to sell? Will you ask your parents or siblings to donate items? Will you ask neighbors if you can sell their items and offer them some of the profits? If your sale is not at your house, how will you get all the items to your sale site?

If you do not live in a house or your neighborhood would not be a good spot for a yard sale, you might be able to get permission to use the grounds of a local school. They might let you use the gym or cafeteria, too, on a rainy day.

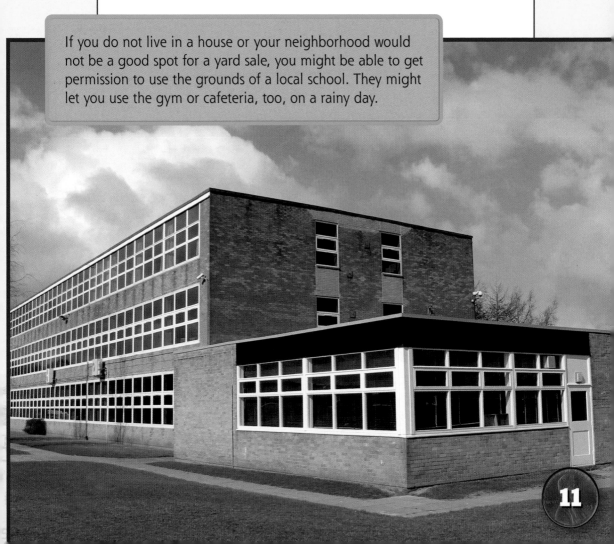

A Budget Is Key

Make a list of your expected expenses and how much you estimate they will be. Be sure to update your budget with the actual numbers once you know them.

Expense Budget	
Tables and chairs	$50.00
Price Stickers (100 count)	$5.00
Site Rental for 3 Hours	$50.00
Advertising Supplies	$15.00
Total	**$120.00**

A **budget** states how much money you plan to spend on your business, exactly what you plan to spend it on, and how much you **estimate** you will make. All entrepreneurs have to spend money to make money. You want to keep your **expenses** low in order to maximize your profits, though.

Make a list of all the things you will need to buy for your yard sale and estimate how much they will cost. These are your expenses. Next, think about how much money you already have.

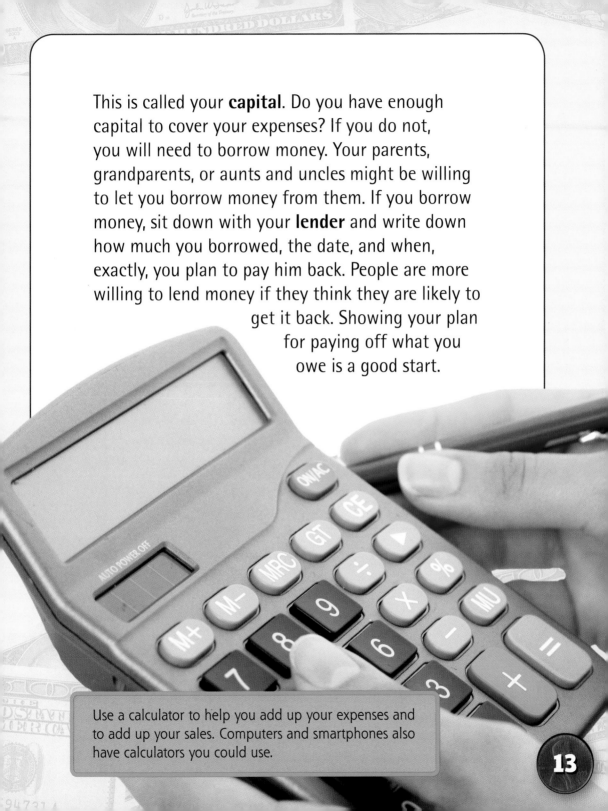

This is called your **capital**. Do you have enough capital to cover your expenses? If you do not, you will need to borrow money. Your parents, grandparents, or aunts and uncles might be willing to let you borrow money from them. If you borrow money, sit down with your **lender** and write down how much you borrowed, the date, and when, exactly, you plan to pay him back. People are more willing to lend money if they think they are likely to get it back. Showing your plan for paying off what you owe is a good start.

Use a calculator to help you add up your expenses and to add up your sales. Computers and smartphones also have calculators you could use.

Be aware that your lender might charge you interest, even if the lender is a parent. Interest is a little extra money that the lender requests as a sort of fee for loaning money.

Save the **receipts** and keep a list of everything you buy and exactly how much it cost. Compare this list to your budget frequently to make sure you're not spending too much.

You will want to keep track of your income as well as your expenses. Record how much you make for each yard sale you hold. Your business is a success if you are covering your expenses and making some profits as well.

Maybe you will decide to offer refreshments at your yard sale. Be sure to include the cost of those supplies in your budget.

Advertise! Advertise!

No one will come to your yard sale if people don't know you're having it! You'll want to devote some of your budget to advertising. Advertising serves two purposes. The first is to let people know where and when you will be holding the yard sale. The second is to point out any special items you are selling. You might make signs that say, "Baseball cards, $1 per box!" or "Big selection of Halloween costumes!"

Make sure your signs are readable and that they have all the information a person needs to find your sale. You may want to protect your signs from weather by putting them between two sheets of clear contact paper and trimming any extra.

Be creative with your signs. A sign at your site will make it easy for people to know they have come to the right place for your yard sale.

Consider what sort of advertising is within your reach and budget. You probably can't afford a billboard on the highway, but you might be able to buy some pieces of big poster board and thick permanent markers with which to make signs. Write the "what," "where," and "when" of your yard sale in big, clear letters and decorate the signs with glitter, ribbons, or balloons to attract people's attention. Then hang the signs on street corners, trees, or telephone poles in your neighborhood. You can put flyers in your neighbors' mailboxes and ask your friends to do the same in their neighborhoods. Many local businesses have places to post community news. Ask if you can hang a flyer there. The library, post office, and convenience stores are just a few places to consider.

Think about making your sign in a fun shape to catch people's attention.

Find out what it costs to print a small ad in your local newspaper. If it is not too costly, this can be a great way to get the word out to a larger audience.

Tip Central

Some cities and towns have rules about where people can put up signs. Before you hang up yours, ask a parent to help you find the number for your local city office and ask about rules for sign display. You don't want to wake up one morning and find that someone has taken all your great signs down.

The library can be a good place to post community events. Ask your librarian if you can hang one of your posters in the library the next time you are there.

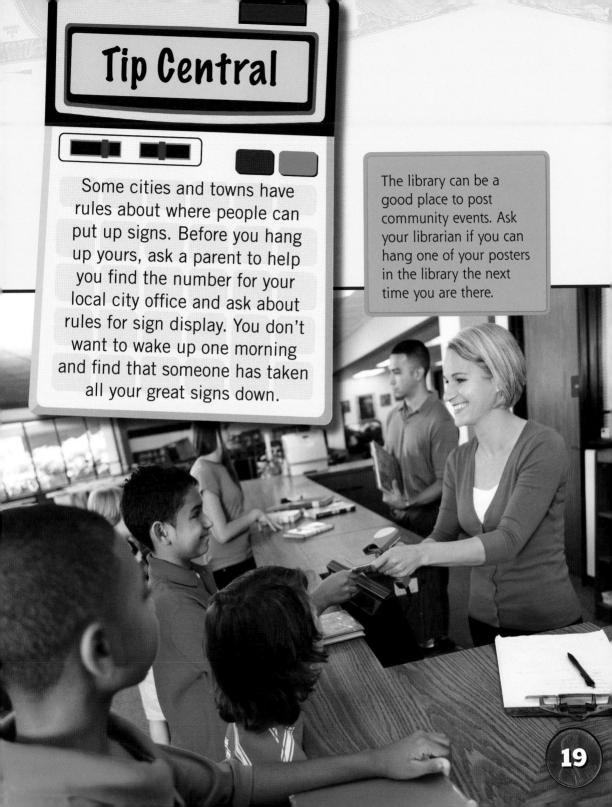

19

Supply Yourself

Make a list of all the supplies you will need for your sale. Include everything from materials to create your signs or flyers, to tables and chairs for the actual day, to the items you will sell. Think about how you will price the items for sale. Will you put stickers on each individual item? Maybe you will decide to group things by price and put one sign on each table instead. Whatever you decide, be sure to include the supplies you will need on your list.

How many tables will you need? Can you borrow them or do you need to buy or rent some? Will you use tablecloths? Do you have a cash box? You will need a safe place to store all the money you make from the sale. It is also a good idea to get lots of $1 and $5 bills and coins for your sale so that you can make change for customers. Be sure to pay yourself or your parents back at the end of the sale for the money you put into the cash box.

Make a box for donated toys and household items and then let your neighbors and friends know you are happy to collect their unwanted items.

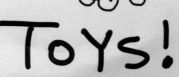

DONATION TOYS

TOYS!

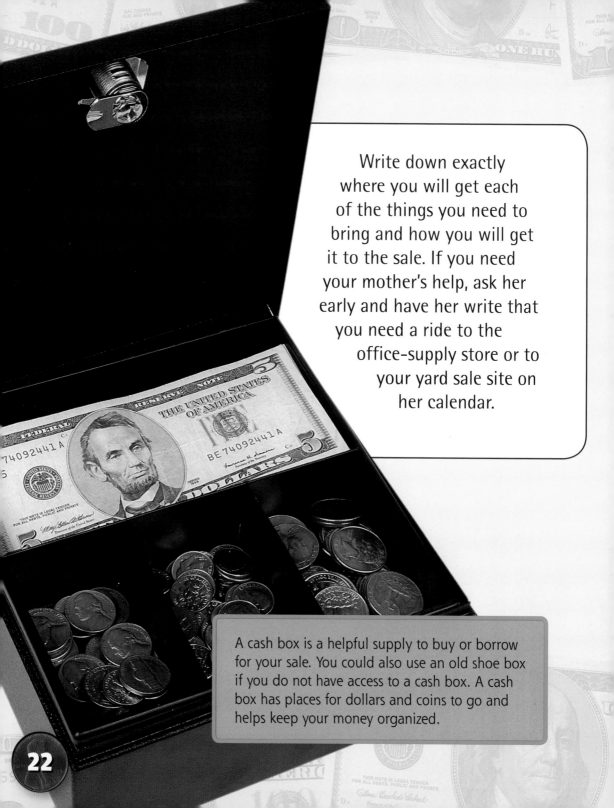

Write down exactly where you will get each of the things you need to bring and how you will get it to the sale. If you need your mother's help, ask her early and have her write that you need a ride to the office-supply store or to your yard sale site on her calendar.

A cash box is a helpful supply to buy or borrow for your sale. You could also use an old shoe box if you do not have access to a cash box. A cash box has places for dollars and coins to go and helps keep your money organized.

Don't forget, you need a place to store all these items in the days leading up to the sale, too. Offer to organize the garage or a closet at home to make room for your supplies.

You will need a notebook to make lists and stay organized, as well as supplies to make posters and thumbtacks to put them up. Put your supplies in one place so you know exactly where to look when you need something.

Power in Numbers

Assign a friend or a sibling to be in charge of the cash box. You should choose a person who is pretty good at math or who knows how to use a calculator.

You don't just need signs, tables, and things to sell at your yard sale. You are probably going to need some people, too. These are your **human resources**. With other people's help, you can gather more items to sell, advertise more widely, and hold a longer, bigger sale.

Of course, you will have to pay your helpers. You can do this one of three ways. You can offer them an hourly wage, maybe $5 per hour, for instance. You could pay them a flat fee, such as $25, to help you for the whole day. You could also offer your help a portion of the profits, such as 5 or 10% of however much money the sale brings in.

If you decide to ask friends to help, show them your plan and what jobs you need filled. Let them choose jobs that interest them, or assign them jobs based on what you know they are good at.

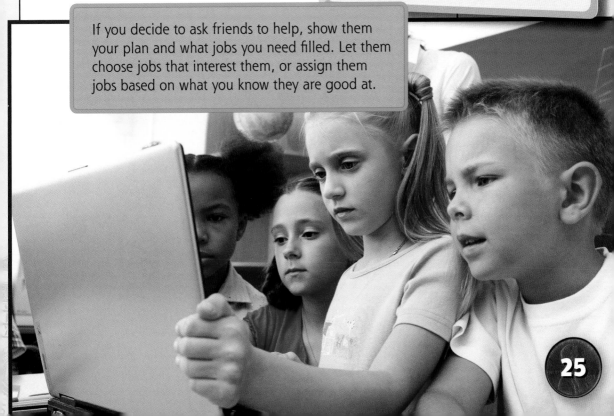

Your Very Own Yard Sale

It's the big day! You'll want to get started early. Setting up the tables the day before could save time on the day of the sale. Be sure your venue will let you do this, and check that the weather will cooperate with this plan. Have your helpers carry out the tables you need to display your items. Set up the tables far enough apart that people can circulate around them.

You have worked hard on your yard sale. Remember to smile at your customers and have fun.

Make sure you make your price tags clear and easy to read. Keep in mind, too, that many people like to haggle, or try to get a lower price, at yard sales. Mark items with prices slightly higher than what you want to get for them so you can still make money.

Then arrange the items you are selling. Do this on the day of the sale, not the day before, though. Remember that people are more likely to buy things if you display them neatly and attractively. You should also mark the prices, using pieces of masking tape or stickers.

If you have decided to have people help you, give each person a specific job. These might include recording purchases in a notebook, taking money and making change, and carrying large items to people's cars. Be sure to keep careful track of all the money going out and coming in. Keep the money in a cash box, rather than your pocket, so you do not lose it.

After the sale, don't forget to clean up. Return or donate the items that did not sell and return the tables you used. Count your money carefully, and make sure that the amount in the cash box matches the amount recorded in the notebook.

Pay your helpers the amount you agreed on and pay back any money you may have borrowed. Anything left over is yours to keep. Enjoy your profits!

If you think you want to hold more yard sales in the future, be sure to practice good customer service so people will come back. Smile and thank your customers as you take their payment.